THE LITTLE MIXER

By

LILLIAN NICHOLSON SHEARON

INDIANAPOLIS
THE BOBBS-MERRILL COMPANY
PUBLISHERS

Printed in the United States of America

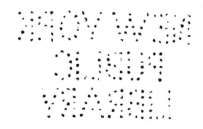

PRESS OF
BRAUNWORTH & CO.
BOOK MANUFACTURERS
BROOKLYN, N. Y.

THE LITTLE MIXER

THE LITTLE MIXER

THERE was no fault to be found
with the present itself; the
trouble lay in the method of trans-
portation. This thought was definite
enough in Hannah's mind, but she
had to rely upon a seven-year-old vo-
cabulary for expression, and grown-
ups are notably dull of comprehen-
sion. Even mothers don't always
understand without being told ex-
actly in so many words.

"I didn't say the kimono wasn't

nice, Mama," explained Hannah, "and 'course Cousin Carrie was awful good to send it to me, but— but Santy Claus is going to bring Virginia one to-morrow night, *down the chimbley!*"

Rose Joseph slipped the absurd little garment over her daughter's dainty lingerie frock, and stood her on a chair that she might view herself in the narrow mirror between the windows of the living-room. The child was as lovely as a flower, but vanity was still sound asleep in her soul, and she glanced indifferently at the reflection, her body sagging with disappointment. "It is just like those little Japanese girls wear," her mother cried in that over-enthusiastic adult tone which warns a child he is about to be the recipient of a gold brick. "I am sure Virginia's can't be any nicer than this one!"

"But, Mama, Santy Claus is going to bring hers *down the chimbley*. Mine"—her voice dropped to a mournful key—"mine came *through the door!*"

"But, darling, what difference does that make just so you get it?"

Pity for her mother's barren child-

hood shone in Hannah's soft black
eyes. "That's—that's no way for
presents to come," she explained;
"Mama, it's Chris'mus."

"It is Chanuca," Mrs. Joseph responded firmly. "Remember you are
a Jewess, dear."

"I can't never forget it," said the
child with a catch in her voice,
" 'specially at Chris'mus."

"But, darling, the Jewish children
have Chanuca; it comes about the
same time as Christmas, and amounts
to the same thing."

Hannah shook her bronze curls.
"Chanuca is because the children of

Israel took Jerusalem and the temple
away from the bad people," she recited glibly, "and—and you say
prayers, and light candles—eight
days, and—and all your uncles and
aunts and cousins send you things,
but Santy Claus, he don't pay any
'tention to Chanuca.   Chris'mus
is just one day, and Santy Claus
comes down the chimbley and brings
things to all good children—'cept
little Jews—because it is the birthday
of our Saviour."

Mrs. Joseph was silent so long
that Hannah felt she had convinced
her mother of the superiority of the

Gentile Christmas over the Jewish Chanuca, and she continued more in detail. "And the children's kinfolks just give Santy Claus money, and tell him what to buy, and he brings the presents, and nobody has to bother about it 'cept him."

"Hannah," Mrs. Joseph interrupted coldly, "who told you about the birthday of—of the Saviour?"

"Nellie Halloran," answered Hannah, "and Virginia, too. They've—they've got the same one."

"The same what?"

"The same Saviour," Hannah explained.

"Darling, hasn't Mama told you many times, that you must never, never talk about religion to Nellie and Virginia?"

"Oh, we don't, Mama, never, never! But 'course we got to talk about Santy Claus, and things."

There seemed to be no reasonable objection to that, so Mrs. Joseph dropped the subject. She spent a great deal of time folding the despised and rejected kimono into its tissue-paper wrappings. Presently she brought a narrow parcel from another room.

"See what Uncle Aaron has sent

you, dear," she cried gaily. "A little man; you wind him up in the back with this key—so—and then he dances and plays the fiddle!"

Hannah forced a polite giggle at the little man's antics. He too rested under the ban of having come "through the door," and her attention soon wandered.

"Nellie got a jumping-jack in the very top of her stocking last Chris'-mus; 'cause she's such a jumping-jack herself, her papa said. You know, Mama, Santy Claus puts nuts and candy, and *little* things in your stocking and puts your big things all

around the room. Sometimes he
brings a tree and hangs them all on
a tree. Virginia and Nellie want a
tree and a new doll. Virginia gets a
new doll every Chris'mus, and she's
got every doll Santy ever brought
her—even her little, baby, rubber
doll. She's eight years old and will
have eight dolls! But Nellie ain't
—hasn't saved a single one, and she's
scared she won't get one this Chris'-
mus—awful scared."

"Why, dear?" asked Mrs. Joseph,
when Hannah paused for breath.

"Because the doll Santy brought
Nellie last Chris'mus, you know

what? She was playing Indian with her brother one day, and *chopped her head off!* And Nellie's mama says she don't know whether old Santy's going to forget that or *not!* But Nellie, she says she prays hard to the Virgin Mary every night—if she don't go to sleep too quick. Mama, what's a virgin? Mama, what's—"

"A virgin is a lady who has never been married," answered Mrs. Joseph, putting the neglected musician back into his box.

Hannah wrestled alone for a moment with a mighty ecclesiastical problem, and then gave it up.

"The Virgin Mary is God's mother," Hannah continued. "That's her picture over our fireplace,"— pointing to a copy of a crude thirteenth century Madonna and Child in a carved Gothic frame, which Eli and Rose Joseph had bought in Italy while on their wedding trip. Flanked now by candles burning in silver candelabra in honor of Chanuca, it gave the mantel a passing resemblance to a Catholic shrine.

"I don't think God's mother is very pretty, do you, Mama? And I think Nellie's little brother is a heap prettier'n God was when He was a baby."

Mrs. Joseph showed signs of having reached the limit. "Hannah," she said firmly, "it is time you were in bed."

"But, Papa hasn't come home yet."

"Papa will be late to-night, dear."

"The Chris'mus rush," sighed Hannah. "Mama, you haven't looked down my throat to-day," she added, playing for time.

Mrs. Joseph went through the daily ritual. "It looks all right," she pronounced.

"It *is* all right," came the triumphant answer. "It is never going to be sore again. Virginia says——"

"Never mind what Virginia says. If your throat ever hurts you the least little bit, you are to come to me instantly and tell me. Do you understand?"

"Yes, Mama, but it isn't going to hurt any more," Hannah insisted.

"Come on up-stairs to bed."

Still Hannah hung back. She had not played her trump card yet, and the time was short. She caught her mother's slim white hand in hers and fingered nervously at the rings. "Mama," she almost whispered, "Virginia says it's Jewish mamas' fault that Santy Claus don't come to see Jewish children. If the mamas would just go to Santy and *tell* him to come— You will, won't you, Mama? *Please, Mama!*"

"Hannah, not another word about Christmas and Santy Claus—not—another—word!"

Hannah swallowed something that came in her throat, and bravely winked back her tears. "Can't Mandy put me to bed?"

"No, dear; Mandy is busy in the kitchen. Mama will put you to bed and tell you stories." She bent down and kissed the child tenderly.

Hannah flung her arms about her

mother's neck. She loved the feel of the soft throat and the gently curving bosom against her little cheek, and the fragrance of her mother's hair and silken laces. She didn't know that her mother looked like a portrait by Raphael, but she did know that her mama was the prettiest, sweetest mama in all the world; and yet——

"Mama, I'm so tired of stories about the children of Israel. They never did anything funny. Mandy tells me tales about the old plan-tashun, when her ma was a slave, and about ole Marse, and ole Mis' going to town and giving Santy Claus money so's he'd bring beads and 'juice' harps and things to the little niggers; and he never forgot one, from the biggest to the littlest darky, Santy didn't."

The child's body began to tremble with repressed sobs. "I—I wisht I was a—a little darky! It's—it's awful—sad to be a little Jewish child at Chris'mus time."

And then the storm broke.

Two hours later Eli Joseph's tired step sounded on the veranda, and Rose hurried to admit him, lifting a silencing hand as soon as he had crossed the threshold. "Hannah has just gone to sleep," she whispered. "No—no, she's not sick at all." He placed an arm around her and drew her into the library.

"Eli, your overcoat is wet," she exclaimed, untwining her arms from his neck.

"Snow," he said, his good-looking boyish face lighting up with pleasure. "It seems we are to have a white Christmas after all."

"Christmas!" she cried; "I wish I could never hear that word again."

"Well, I'm glad it comes only once a year. To-night ends my siege, though. To-morrow night Stein goes on duty, and I come home for dinner to stay. Rose, darling, you look all tired out. You shouldn't wait up for me."

"It isn't that. It's Hannah. She cried for more than an hour to-night, and but for Mandy and her tales I believe she would still be crying." And she detailed the scene to him.

"But, good gracious, Rose, let Santa Claus bring her presents to her," said Eli, when she had finished. "Hannah's nothing but a baby."

"She is beginning to think for herself."

"As you did at a very early age,"

he reminded her, "and your father the strictest of orthodox rabbis. How old were you when you began slipping off to the reformed temple?"

"I broke my father's heart," she said somberly. "I'll be punished through Hannah."

"Not unless you let Hannah think faster than you do. And remember," he added teasingly, "if you hadn't run off to the reformed temple you would never have met me."

"Outside, at the foot of the steps," she recalled. "I would never have met you inside."

"Maybe I am lax," he acknowledged, "but it seems to me that if you are living a decent life yourself, and giving the other fellow a square deal, you are pretty nearly fulfilling the law and the prophets."

"And what do you suppose is happening to Hannah with a Christian Science family on one side and Roman Catholics on the other?" she demanded tragically. "She's decided not to take any more medicine, because Virginia Lawrence doesn't. And she has Nellie Halloran's every expression about the Virgin and the Saviour. Not only that, but she has made friends with a Christian Science practitioner through the Lawrences, and calls him 'my friend Mr. Jackson.' She runs to meet him and walks the length of the block with him every time he passes."

"Hannah is certainly a natural born mixer," laughed the father. "We are saving ourselves trouble by giving her the best there is to mix with!"

"Eli, I am afraid we made a mistake moving out here, away from all our people."

"No, we didn't make a mistake," he declared earnestly. "The Square was no place to bring up Hannah,

among those parvenu Jews. We have
the prettiest home on the heights and
the best people in town for neighbors."

"Our child is losing her identity as
a Jewess."

"Let her find it again as an Ameri-
can," he replied. "Frankly, Rose, I
don't lose any sleep over trying to
keep *my* identity as a Jew intact. If
a Jew doesn't like it here, let him go
back to Palestine or to the country
that oppressed him, I say. I've got the
same amount of patience with these
hyphenated Americans as I have with
the Jews who try to segregate themselves and dot the map with New

Jerusalems.   Where's the sense in throwing yourself into the melting-pot, glad of the chance, and then kicking because you come out something different?—Come on to bed, dear; you are as pale as a ghost, and I'm so tired I can't see straight.   Our baby is all right.   Don't you worry."

Snow falls on the just and the unjust.   There was quite as much of it in Hannah's back yard as in either Virginia's or Nellie's—perhaps even a little more had drifted into the fence corners.   Hannah's joy in discovering that in this respect she had not been slighted crowded her troubles into the background. Immediately after breakfast, bundled up snugly, she stood in her yard and threw snowballs toward her neighbors' homes, while she squealed with delight. In a very few minutes, three little girls were playing where only one had played before.

The two newcomers, Virginia Lawrence and Nellie Halloran, presented an interesting contrast. Virginia, slim, and tall for her age, with long, flat, yellow braids, handled the snow daintily, even gingerly. Nellie, fat and dimpled, her curls tousled

into a flame colored halo, rolled over
and over in the snow, and then shook
herself like a puppy. Until the ad-
vent of Hannah, a subtle antagonism
had existed between the two children.
Virginia's favorite game was playing
"lady" with a train floating grace-
fully behind her; Nellie's chief joy
in life was seeing how long she could
stand on her head, her short skirts
obeying the laws of gravity all the
while. Hannah, however, vibrated
obligingly between the two sports,
and kept the peace inviolate.

Romping in the snow is hard play,
and presently the little girls sat pant-

ing on the top step of the Josephs' back porch. Immediately Nellie produced a string of amethyst colored beads from her coat pocket, with the announcement that she would say her prayers while resting.

"What kind of beads are those?" asked Hannah.

"Rosary beads, 'course," responded Nellie. "Hannah, you don't know anything."

"I do, too."

"Huh! you didn't even know about the Mother o' God until I told you."

"I reckon I thought God was an orphan," Hannah pleaded in extenua-

tion. "But, what about God's papa?"
she demanded with sudden inspira-
tion. "You're so smarty, tell me
about that!"

"Oh, God didn't have to have a
father," Nellie answered easily.
"Everything is free in Heaven; so
He didn't have to have a father to
work for Him when He was little."

"Then why did He have to have a
mama?"

"To tell Him what to do, 'course.
You know how 'tis. If you ask your
papa anything, don't he always say,
'Go ask your mama'?"

Hannah had noticed this shifting

of masculine responsibility more than once. "That's so," she acquiesced. Then a terrible thought struck her. "I don't want to go to Heaven! I don't want to go anywhere unless my papa can go too."

Nellie's nimble Irish wits were ready. "I just said *God* didn't need any papa. 'Course *our* papas will go to Heaven, 'cause that's the only place they can quit working. Didn't I hear my papa say one time he hoped he'd get a little rest in Heaven, 'cause he never got any on this earth?"

"But, you have to die before you can get to Heaven," sighed Hannah.

Virginia, who had been maintaining a most dignified silence, looked as if she must speak or explode. "No you don't. Heaven begins here and now," she recited. "If you are good, you are well and happy, and that's Heaven."

" 'Tisn't," scoffed Nellie. "Do you see any angels flying 'round in this here yard? I don't."

Hannah rather took to Virginia's argument, and resolved to have conversation with her some time, undampened by Nellie's skepticism. If there could be feasting on the joys of Heaven here and now,

Hannah had every intention of being at the banquet table. At the present moment, however, the rosary beads were of fascinating interest; she must hold them in her own hands, and watch the play of purple lights upon the snow as she flashed them in the sun. Questions about the crucifix, she found, brought on an embarrassing silence. Nellie looked at Virginia. Virginia looked at Nellie. Then the two excused themselves for a whispered colloquy at the other end of the yard. When they returned, Virginia acted as spokesman, fixing Nellie with an unrelenting eye.

"That is Jesus nailed to the cross, Hannah.   Some very wicked people did it."

There was nothing exciting in this to Hannah; wicked people were doing wicked things the world over, all the time.   The statement fell flat, and Nellie, disappointed at the lack of dramatic effect, broke treaty.   "I 'spect the Jews did it," she said.

"They did not!"   Hannah's voice trembled.   "The Jews are nice people; they wouldn't do a wicked thing like that!"

Virginia put an arm across Hannah's shoulders.   "Now see what you've done," she snapped at Nellie.

"Oh, I 'spect the Irish helped them," Nellie added magnanimously. "My papa says the Irish are into every thing."

Not having to bear the ignominy alone Hannah was comforted. "What makes you say prayers on the beads?" she asked.

" 'Cause I want Santy to bring me a doll to-night. I wrote him 'bout sixteen letters, and I'm going to say my rosary a dozen times to-day."

To-morrow was Christmas Day! Hannah's face fell. All her sorrows returned with a rush. "Have you got any more of those beads?" she asked.

"Yes, but they wouldn't do you any good," Nellie answered with quick understanding. "You're not a Catholic."

"Couldn't I be one?"

"Not unless you're baptized with holy water. The priest does it."

The leaven had begun to work.

"What did your mama say about asking Santa Claus to come?" Virginia inquired, with a quick glance toward the beads.

Hannah shook her head, speechless. She compressed her lips into a tight line with an effort at self-control, but two large tears rolled down her cheeks and splashed on her scarlet coat. Again Virginia placed an arm protectingly across Hannah's shoulder.

Nellie's bright blue eyes grew soft with pity. "I tell you what," she exclaimed. "I'll baptize Hannah, then she'll be a Gentile, and Santa Claus will come, no matter what. And when your mama sees how nice it is, she won't care."

"But, you said a priest has to baptize anybody," objected Virginia.

"He does 'less it's a time of danger and you can't get any priest.

Then any Catholic can baptize anybody. My mama baptized our wash-
erwoman's little baby 'cause they
knew it was going to die before
Father Murphy could get there. And
ain't this a time of danger?"

"Nobody's dying." Virginia was
distressingly literal.

Hannah looked from one friend to
the other, hoping against hope.

"No, but there's danger Santa
Claus won't come to see Hannah
less'n sump'n is done mighty quick,"
came Nellie's ready reply. "And
can we get a priest? You go get one,
Virginia. Go get one."

Clearly there was no answer to this. The ceremony was set for early afternoon when Grandmother Halloran took her nap and Nellie could borrow the bottle of holy water from her shelf. As to the place, there were six boys at the Hallorans' always in the way; Mrs. Lawrence had guests; obviously the baptismal rite would have to be performed at Hannah's home. After lunch the children assembled in the sun parlor of the Josephs' home, in full view of Mrs. Joseph who sat embroidering in the library, the French door closed between them, so that she did not hear.

Nellie had secured the bottle of holy water, and, arrayed in her brother Joe's long, black rain-coat, a towel about her neck for a stole, acted as priest. Virginia, not to be left out of such an important affair, consented to be godmother. In lieu of a prayer manual, Nellie used one of Hannah's story books. She chose a verse, which, because she knew it by heart, she could read exceptionally well:

"Little boy blue, come blow your
    horn,
The sheep are in the meadow,
And the cows are in the corn."

Then she poured a little of the holy water on Hannah's forehead (wet hair might occasion unanswerable questions) and baptized her "Hannah Agnes Ignatius Joseph."

Called upon for a response, the godmother recited very impressively the Scientific Statement of Being as found in the Christian Science text-book, and Hannah was pronounced a Gentile and a Catholic.

One thing more remained to be done. Hannah ran to her mother, cheeks aglow. "Mama, may I trade my striped ball to Nellie for some beads?"

"Why of course, darling, if you wish."

The exchange was made, and some time was spent in mastering the use of the rosary. All three of the children knew the "Our Father," though there was some difference of opinion as to "debts" and "trespasses" which is apt to hold in all mixed congregations. The "Hail Mary" proved a bit difficult for Hannah, and she finally abandoned it. "I'll say, 'Hear, oh Israel, the Lord our God, the Lord is One,'" she said. "I already know that, and a prayer is a prayer, isn't it?"

Nellie refilled the holy-water bottle from the kitchen hydrant, and hurried home to replace it before her grandmother should awaken. Hannah spent the next hour lying flat on her stomach printing letters, appealing to Virginia from time to time for aid as to the spelling, Virginia being a very superior speller.

Mrs. Joseph was busy with callers when Virginia went home, and Hannah was left to her own devices. Suddenly she thought of one stone that had been left unturned: there was her friend Mr. Jackson to whom the Lawrences always appealed in time of stress. She knew the formula, she knew his number, for on the list by the Lawrences' telephone, his name, like Abou-ben-Adhem's, led all the rest. "Main 1234," it was as easy as counting. She slipped into the telephone closet and closed the door.

There was no trouble with Hannah that night. She went to bed early, and didn't care to have any stories told—she could go to sleep by herself.

"Quite a change of heart, eh?" Eli commented to Rose, as they sat by the living-room fire after telling their little girl good night.

"She has been like that all day, playing as happily as you please," Rose responded. "I suppose she got it all out of her system in last night's scene."

Eli drummed abstractedly on the arm of his chair: "I don't feel quite right about it, even so," he said.

"Maybe you will think me inconsistent," she confessed, flushing, "but Hannah was so indifferent about the presents sent her for Chanuca, I only showed her two. I've saved the others to give her Christmas Day, so she will have something of her own to show when the other children bring theirs over."

Eli didn't seem any too pleased.
"Poor little mite," he murmured.

"His-st! Missis Joseph!"

It was Bridget, the Hallorans' old
family servant, calling softly from
the hall.

"I'll be after takin' the prisints
ye've stored away for us. I'll lave
'em on the back porch 'n' carry 'em
over when the childer are all asleep.
Nellie's in bed like a little angel,
bless 'er heart, but them divilish b'ys
do be a-snoopin' into ivery crack 'n'
corner!"

Mrs. Joseph unlocked a closet

under the stairs, and loaded Bridget's arms with heavy and bulky parcels.

"Shure, an' 'tis a sad Chris'mus we'll be havin', savin' the childer. Mr. Timmy, him that's old Missis Halloran's youngest, but old enough to know better, he ups an' runs away to-day an' marries a Protestant gir-rl. An' if ye'll open y'r windy the bit av a crack, ye'll hear the poor old lady this minit, wailin' like a banshee."

"But Mr. Timothy is such a nice young man, he must have married a lovely girl, Bridget," said Rose.

"Shure, an' that may be, but she is a Protestant, Missis Joseph. She

runs away fr'm her folks, an' he runs
away fr'm his, an' they get married
by a justice o' peace. An' no peace
will come o' such doin', Lord 've
mercy on their souls!"

"Oh, poor Grandma Halloran!"

"Poor lovers," said Eli, when
Bridget had gone. "I'll wager they
had the very deuce of a time with
both sides."

No sooner had they settled themselves again than the door knocker
sounded. Eli admitted Mr. Jackson,
the Christian Science practitioner.

"I have only a minute," he said.
"I just dropped by to leave a doll my

wife dressed for your little girl. We chose one that we thought looked like Hannah."

"Oh, but that is kind of you!" Rose looked her gratitude. "Mrs. Lawrence has told me how busy both you and your wife always are— and to take time to think of our little girl——!"

"I had intended to give it to her myself," Mr. Jackson continued, "but after her talk with me to-day I decided she would enjoy it more if I asked Santa Claus to bring it." His eyes twinkled reminiscently. "She called me up by telephone and asked me to give Santa Claus a treatment—she seemed to think that he would pass her by. I could assure her that he wouldn't, as I had already seen the doll. Hannah is a wonderful child."

"We think so," smiled Eli. "I am sure we thank you, and wish you the very merriest Christmas."

"It will be a *happy* Christmas for me," he answered. "I am going to the station to meet my father and mother. Some years ago they felt estranged from me—they are both staunch Presbyterians of the old school and it nearly broke their hearts when I went into Christian Science work. But they are beginning to look more tolerantly upon my calling, and they are on their way now to spend Christmas with us. You can guess how happy that makes me. 'Peace on earth, good will to men'—it is a wonder-working thought."

"It is indeed," Eli agreed heartily.

When the door had closed upon their visitor, Rose and Eli stood staring at each other rather foolishly. She was the first to speak: "Is there no end to the fight between the old and the new generation?"

"We are just beginning the scrap with *our* new generation," he said. "She called him up and asked for Christian Science help! I wonder what else that little monkey has been up to?"

They soon found out. Carrying the doll Mr. Jackson had brought, Rose tiptoed after Eli into the nursery and gradually turned on the light. The first object to meet their eyes was Hannah's stocking, hanging precariously to a pin driven into the mantel. Pinned to the wall were several messages, neatly printed in pencil, which told their own tale:

Deer Santy—Nellie babtized me.
Holy wotter.   Hannah.

Deer Santy—I want things in my
stockin.   Hannah.

Deer Santy, Claws—Ime a jentile.
Nellie babtize me.   Ime a jentile
cath-lic C. S.   Hannah.

Deer Santy—Bring me any nice
things you got left.   With love
                        Hannah.

Deer Santy—Don't let my Mama
and my Papa get mad bout you.
                        Hannah.

Eli began to chortle, and Hannah
stirred in her sleep, throwing both
chubby arms over her head. Clutched
tightly in her left hand they saw a
rosary of amethyst colored beads.

Rose snapped off the light and
pushed Eli out into the hall. He sat

down on the stairs and laughed until he cried. "The dog-gone little mixer!" he chuckled. "A Gentile Catholic Christian Scientist is she? And if she has ever happened to hear anything about Mahomet, believe me, she's sleeping with her feet toward Mecca right now!"

Rose was weeping silently over the little message: "Don't let my Mama and my Papa get mad bout you." She touched her husband on the shoulder, "Eli, what shall we do about it?"

"Do?" He stood up and set his jaw determinedly. "You spoke just now of the fight between the old and the new generations: do you see what we are coming to if we don't concede our child her legitimate rights. She will seek them out, and take them by force, and never forgive us for withholding them, that's what! Every child who has ever heard of Santa Claus has a right to enjoy the myth. Didn't I give a hundred dollars to the Elks and a hundred dollars to the Big Brothers who are looking after the empty stockings of the poor children, while my own baby——"

He had reached his bedroom door

and was kicking off his house slip-
pers.

"Eli, where are you going?"

"Down-town to see Santa Claus if
I have to break open a dozen stores,"
he answered determinedly.

It seemed that Santa Claus, never
having visited Hannah before, had a
mind to make up for lost time. An
overflowing stocking hung from the
mantel; a tree loaded with presents
and tinsel stood by her bed; about the
room were placed large gifts, everything a little girl might wish for.
Hannah was dazed. She didn't see

her mother and father standing in
the doorway of the nursery, their
arms about each other, and smiling.
She tugged at her window until it
opened and then called to Nellie
across the intervening space.

"He came! He came!" she
screamed, as a tousled, flame-colored
head showed at the window opposite.

Hannah brushed by her parents
and, running to the window nearest
Virginia's room, repeated her message. Then she came back into the
nursery, still oblivious of mother and
father, and stared about her in
ecstasy. The occasion called for

'some expression of thanksgiving— what could it be? A seven-year-old child hasn't words for such a big emotion. She could think of but one thing to do.

Reverently bowing her little bronze head, she made the sign of the cross —upside down!

THE END

CPSIA information can be obtained
at www.ICGtesting.com
Printed in the USA
BVHW090422281021
620061BV00001B/20